The Fourth Watch

A
Watch for Prophets, Warriors,
Intercessors, & Lovesick
Believers

Catrina J. Sparkman

The Fourth Watch

A Watch for Prophets, Warriors, Intercessors & Lovesick Believers

Copyright © 2018 Catrina J. Sparkman

ISBN 13: 978-1-949958-08-9

Paperback edition

All rights reserved. No part of this book may be reproduced, stored in whole or in part or transmitted in any form by any means, without prior written permission from the publisher, except in the case of brief quotations embodied in articles for review. Nor can this book be circulated in any form of binding or cover other than that in which it is published.

All Bible Scriptures taken from the following translations: New International Standard Version, God's Word Translation, English Standard Version, Holman Christian Standard Version, and The King James Version.

Other Books by Catrina J. Sparkman

Non Fiction

Doing Business with God

Intimacy the Beginning of Authority

Divine Revelation for a Twitter Generation

Doing Battle with the Names of God

Intercession the Heartbeat of God

Fiction:

The Redemption's Price Series:

Passing through Water

Opening the Floodgates

The Fire This Time

Table of Contents

Author's Note-1

Chapter 1
What in the World is Going on at 3'oclock in the Morning -6

Chapter 2
The Biblical Relevance of the 4th Watch -9

Chapter 3
What Happens in the Spirit Realm When the People of God Pray During the 4th Watch-17

Chapter 4
The Benefits of Praying During the 4th Watch- 27

Chapter 5
What Should You Bring with You to the 4th Watch? - 29

Chapter 6
Guidelines for Orderly Corporate Prayer-33

Chapter 7
How Should One Prepare for the 4th Watch? - 40

Chapter 8
How Can You Bring the 4th Watch to Your Church or City? - 42

Appendix A
Glossary of Terms Used in Intercession-44

Appendix B

The History of Biblical Anointing Oils & Why We Should Use Them Today-52

Appendix C
Watch Notes- 63

AUTHOR'S NOTE

If you picked up this book than you're probably already a believer, so I don't need to convince you of the reality of Christ. What I do want to do, is to convince you of your need to participate in corporate prayer. And by corporate prayer I don't mean praying with folks at your job although that would certainly qualify, I mean joining together with a group of believers for the sole purpose of talking to God.

It is called corporate prayer for two reasons: number one, because it is done in community, and number two, because when the people of God gather together and pray they make legal transactions with Heaven. They conduct the type of business in the heavenly realms that have lifelong implications right here on Earth. Do you realized that every Spirit-filled prayer you ever prayed will remain in the Earth long after you depart this planet for eternity? I want to convince you to do business with God. Furthermore, I want to convince you to do it during a time that most people have literally called the most ungodly hour of the day. The time slot between the hours of 3-6 AM. A time known to intercessors all over the world as the 4th Watch of the morning. A time also known to those who practice occultism as, the witching hour. At the writing of this, myself and a group of intercessors, have been praying at the 4th Watch for the past eleven years. It has tremendously blessed our lives.

For the first four years or so after we were married, my husband and I traveled to and from Milwaukee every Sunday morning to attend Sunday morning service at the church where I grew up. I was ordained in that house, we were married in that house, and I knew that the meat of the Word was being taught there. So, every Sunday morning we would rise at 5AM to be there in time for 7AM service. When our first-born son was born in 2003, the Lord spoke to my husband and said, "It's time for you and your family to set down roots in the city where I have planted you." We visited some local ministries until we came to the place where we are currently members now. The Lord spoke to my husband again and said, "This is the house I've called you to join." We arrived during a pivotal time in the ministry. They were in transition, it was during a time of growth and expansion. The ministry wanted to build. Shortly after we arrived, I was asked to lead the prayer ministry at the church. It was during this season that the Lord began to speak to my heart concerning what He wanted to accomplish in that house. You may hear me use that term "house" as you read in place of the traditional word, church. I do so because Jesus is coming back for one body of believers. One unified Church. There are many houses of God all over the world but together we make up one Church. One morning, as I was preparing for Sunday morning service the Lord began to speak to my heart. He said very simply, "This building plan is from me." Let me back up for a moment and say that when we arrived at the ministry and heard that they wanted to build, I thought nothing of it. Just about every church in America has a building fund. I had never heard of a church who didn't want to expand. The ministry I grew up in has been raising money for the building fund for the last thirty years. As I was getting ready for service that morning, The Lord spoke to my heart and said, "I want you to put your agreement on this building project because this is me." To which I quickly responded, "Okay, God. If you say you want to build here, I put my agreement on it." The Lord nudged me again. This time He said, "I want them to build, but they don't have the capacity to build. The water level of intercession in this house is too low." So I said, "Okay, Lord, what do you want me to do about it?" The Lord spoke to my heart once again, this time He said, "I want you to lay siege over this place for 31 days during the month of October. I want you to rally the intercessors and meet me there at the church from 3 AM to 6 AM to pray." So I did. We came out from 3-6AM every morning for 31 days and we did it. We laid siege over the house in prayer. I was pregnant with my third child at the time and boy, was it hard to get out of my bed at 2:30 AM to make it to the house of God at 3 AM, but we did it. When the 31 days were over I thought wow, we did it! The thing we thought we couldn't do. Thank God it's over! The Spirit of the Lord spoke to my heart again. "It's not over yet. I want you to choose one day, it can be any day of the week that you choose. I want you to come here once a week on that day from 3-6 AM to maintain the ground." My obvious question to the Lord was, "How long do you want us to do that?" The Spirit spoke back to my heart and said, "Until I say quit." That was eleven years ago. He hasn't told us to stop yet and we have been praying at the 4th Watch of the morning ever since. I'm happy to report that the building remodeling project was completed. We rebuilt on the land God had given us and more than doubled our capacity. We prayed for seven years before the building went up. So in other words it took seven years to build it in the Spirit. The building went up in one year's time in the natural and we grew stronger and more confident in our walk.

Here's the thing, even if you don't do it at 3AM, I want you to pray, and I want you to seriously consider participating in some form of corporate prayer. Our cities need this kind of coverage more than ever. After doing this now for so long, I've come to realize that there are certain benefits that come from crying out to God at the 4th Watch of the morning. In this book I'd like to share some of those benefits with you. I'd also like to give you some tools that would help you establish a Watch of your own, should the Lord lead you in that direction.

As you read the pages of this book, prayerfully consider whether God is calling you to establish something along the lines of this in your area or region. Even if you don't feel a leading to pray at 3AM, please answer Heaven's call to pray. God is looking for those who are willing to stand in the gap. (Ezekiel 22:30) Heaven needs to hear your sound. The Earth needs the benefit of your prayers (Romans 8:19). Every day we meet people with problems that no one has the answer to. No one but God. The good news is that He is still on the throne and in the prayer answering business. The best news is that as a believer in Christ, you can access Him anytime you like. So go ahead, change the world by doing business with God.

Sincerely,
Catrina J. Sparkman

1

What in the World is Going on at 3 O'clock in the Morning?

The 4th Watch tends to be a time of tremendous spiritual attack for Christian believers. During the night, Satan, the enemy of our souls, wages his greatest assault on the minds of believers. Seeds of fear, doubt, anxiety, and evil ideas are often planted in the minds of sleeping believers. This also is the time of night when most people experience night terrors, demonic visitations, and what we call "bad dreams". Most violent crimes are committed and the most self-destructive behavior takes place between the hours of 3 AM and 6 AM.

Throughout the ages, 3 AM has been known far and wide as the witching hour. Those who practice occult arts are more active during this time slot then in any other time of the day. They often use this time to incant over waters, churches, regions, and cities. They choose this time to carry out their wicked plans because it is during the night watches that darkness is at the zenith of its authority. This is also the time when those who have been given true authority to speak and decree over our planet are usually nuzzled tightly in their bed and fast asleep. It is also during the 4th Watch of the morning that those involved in witchcraft, and other forms of occult arts, claim to perform their activities through the means of astral projection, and are returning back to their bases (bodies). Sounds strange, I know, yet there have been many testimonies of former witches that have been converted to Christianity telling of their experiences of going outside of their bodies on witchcraft assignments through means of astral projection. Many of these same witches testify that they had to return into their bodies before 6 AM, otherwise they wouldn't have been able to. This is because they would have been shaken out by the dayspring as according to Job 38:12-13:

"Have you ever given orders to the morning,
  or shown the dawn its place,
that it might take the earth by the edges
  and shake the wicked out of it?

As you read this I want you to have a paradigm shift. I literally want you to change your thinking. Why is it strange to us that the children of darkness are more knowledgeable about the heavenly realms when Jesus himself tells us that the children of darkness are more savvy than the children of light? (Luke 16:8) Jesus seems to be looking throughout the ages and making a commentary that is still relevant for our generation today. Dear people of God, even though our Master said it, this ought not be. Why should the children of darkness do the extraordinary and the children of light only be limited to the ordinary?

2

The Biblical Relevance of the 4ᵗʰ Watch

Several significant events happened in the Bible during the 4ᵗʰ Watch. These events give us clues to the power available to believers today when we harness the time slot of 3-6 AM to do business for and with God.

1. Israel is Released from Bondage During the 4ᵗʰ Watch of the Morning.

It was during the 3ʳᵈ watch, or midnight watch, that God struck down all the firstborn of Egypt. However, it was during the 4th watch of the morning that Israel walked out of 430 years of slavery and oppression into their freedom.

At Midnight the Lord struck down all the firstborn in the land of Egypt, from the firstborn of Pharaoh who sat on his throne to the firstborn of the captive who was in the dungeon, and all the firstborn of the livestock. And Pharaoh rose up in the night, he and all his servants and all the Egyptians. And there was a great cry in Egypt, for there was not a house where someone was not dead. Then he summoned Moses and Aaron by night and said, "up, go out from among my people, both you and the people of Israel; and go, serve the Lord, as you have said, and be gone, and bless me also!" The Egyptians were urgent with the people to send them out of the land in haste. For they said, "We shall all be dead."

Exodus 12: 29-33

2. The Israelites Plundered the Egyptians During The 4th Watch of the Morning.

Not only did they leave but they left with back pay and damages. An estimated 2.5-3.5 million, men, women and children, walked out of Egypt on foot with their livestock, personal possessions in tow, and their Egyptian slavers possessions.

The Egyptians urged the people to hurry and leave the country. "For otherwise," they said, "we will all die!" So the people took their dough before the yeast was added, and carried it on their shoulders in kneading troughs wrapped in clothing. The Israelites did as Moses instructed and asked the Egyptians for articles of silver and gold and for clothing. The LORD had made the Egyptians favorably disposed toward the people, and they gave them what they asked for; so they plundered the Egyptians.

Exodus 12: 33-36

3. Jesus Walked on Water During the 4th Watch of the Morning.

Immediately Jesus made his disciples get into the boat and go on ahead of him to Bethsaida, while he dismissed the crowd. After leaving them, he went up on a mountainside to pray. Later that night, the boat was in the middle of the lake, and he was alone on land. He saw the disciples straining at the oars, because the wind was against them. Shortly before dawn he went out to them, walking on the lake. He was about to pass by them, but when they saw him walking on the lake, they thought he was a ghost. They cried out, because they all *saw him and were terrified. Immediately he spoke to them and said, "Take courage! It is I. Don't be afraid." Then he climbed into the boat with them, and the wind died down.*

Mark 6:45-51

4. Peter Walked on the Water During the 4th Watch of the Morning.

The Matthew passage recounts the same story as the Mark passage, but it gives us slightly more information. Not only do we see Jesus walking on the water we see that Peter walked on the water as well during the 4th Watch of the morning.

Immediately Jesus made the disciples get into the boat and go on ahead of him to the other side, while he dismissed the crowd. After he had dismissed them, he went up on a mountainside by himself to pray. Later that night, he was there alone, and the boat was already a considerable distance from land, buffeted by the waves because the wind was against it. Shortly before dawn Jesus went out to them, walking on the lake. When the disciples saw him walking on the lake, they were terrified. "It's a ghost," they said, and cried out in fear. But Jesus immediately said to them: "Take courage! It is I. Don't be afraid."

"Lord, if it's you," Peter replied, "tell me to come to you on the water." "Come," he said. Then Peter got down out of the boat, walked on the water and came toward Jesus. But when he saw the wind, he was afraid and, beginning to sink, cried out, "Lord, save me!" Immediately

Jesus reached out his hand and caught him. "You of little faith," he said, "why did you doubt?" And when they climbed into the boat, the wind died down. Then those who were in the boat worshiped him, saying, "Truly you are the Son of God."

Matthew 14:22-33

5. The Shulamite Woman Looked for Her Shepherd King During The 4th Watch of The Morning.

The 4th Watch of the night is also when the Shulamite Woman of Song of Solomon went out combing the streets desperate for her lover, who is both a Shepherd and a King. The 4th Watch is a time that believers are stirred to answer the call of intercession and answer the door for the Shepherd King when he knocks.

All night long on my bed
  I looked for the one my heart loves;
  I looked for him but did not find him.
I will get up now and go about the city,
  through its streets and squares;
I will search for the one my heart loves.
  So I looked for him but did not find him.

The watchmen found me
  as they made their rounds in the city.
  "Have you seen the one my heart loves?"
Scarcely had I passed them
  when I found the one my heart loves.
I held him and would not let him go
  till I had brought him to my mother's house,
  to the room of the one who conceived me.

Song of Solomon 3:1-4

6. The Stone Was Rolled Away from Jesus' Tomb During The 4th Watch of the Morning.

When the Sabbath was over, Mary Magdalene, Mary the mother of James, and Salome bought spices so that they might go to anoint Jesus' body. Very early on the first day of the week, just after sunrise, they were on their way to the tomb and they asked each other, "Who will roll the stone away from the entrance of the tomb?"

But when they looked up, they saw that the stone, which was very large, had been rolled away. As they entered the tomb, they saw a young man dressed in a white robe sitting on the right side, and they were alarmed.

"Don't be alarmed," he said. "You are looking for Jesus the Nazarene, who was crucified. He has risen! He is not here. See the place where they laid him. But go, tell his disciples and Peter, 'He is going ahead of you into Galilee. There you will see him, just as he told you.'"

Trembling and bewildered, the women went out and fled from the tomb. They said nothing to anyone, because they were afraid.

Mark 16: 1-8

7. The Spirit of Pentecost Fell upon the Disciples During the 4th Watch of the Morning.

Believers who had tarried all night waiting for the promised gift met the morning with power.

When the day of Pentecost came, they were all together in one place. Suddenly a sound like the blowing of a violent wind came from heaven and filled the whole house where they were sitting. They saw what seemed to be tongues of fire that separated and came to rest on each of them. All of them were filled with the Holy Spirit and began to speak in other tongues as the Spirit enabled them. Now there were staying in Jerusalem God-fearing Jews from every nation under heaven. When they heard this sound, a crowd came together in bewilderment, because each one heard their own language being spoken. Utterly amazed, they asked: "Aren't all these who are speaking Galileans? Then how is it that each of us hears them in our native language? Parthians, Medes and Elamites; residents of Mesopotamia, Judea and Cappadocia, Pontus and Asia, Phrygia and Pamphylia, Egypt and the parts of Libya near Cyrene; visitors from Rome (both Jews and converts to Judaism); Cretans and Arabs—we hear them declaring the wonders of God in our own tongues!" Amazed and perplexed, they asked one another, "What does this mean?" Some, however, made fun of them and said, "They have had too much wine." Then Peter stood up with the Eleven, raised his voice and addressed the crowd: "Fellow Jews and all of you who live in Jerusalem, let me explain this to you; listen carefully to what I say. These people are not drunk, as you suppose. It's only nine in the morning!

Acts 2:1-15

3

What Happens in the Spirit Realm when the People of God Pray During the 4th Watch?

Based on the scriptures we studied in the last chapter we can expect several things to happen when we meet God during the 4th Watch of the morning.

1. During the 4th Watch God Reveals Himself as the Uncontested King.

In the Exodus 12 and the Mark 6 passages we see God's people in great distress and in need of a savior. Further study of these passages suggest that both Israel and the disciples where being opposed by supernatural forces. In both passages, God sees His people's distress and yet He waits until the 4th Watch of the morning-- when evil is at the height of its authority, to deliver His people. In doing so He proves to those who are for and against Him, that He and He alone is the Uncontested King.

2. During the 4ᵗʰ Watch We Meet Jesus the Deliverer.

Both the book of Exodus and the Mark passage also give us a picture of Jesus as deliverer. In Mark, we clearly see Jesus walking on water to come to the aid of those He loves. And in the book of Exodus we see a picture of the pre-incarnated Christ leading His people out of bondage in the form of a cloud.

By day the Lord went ahead of them in a pillar of cloud to guide them on their way and by night in a pillar of fire to give them light so that they could travel by day or night. Neither the pillar of cloud by day nor the pillar of fire by night left its place in front of the people.

Exodus 13:21-22

What we can take away from these passages is this, Jesus will always be personally involved in the deliverance process. What He did for Israel in the desert and His disciples on the water, He'll do for you. If He has called you to the 4ᵗʰ Watch for a season of healing and deliverance then you need not fear, God has already gone ahead of you and chartered your route of escape. He may be using people to usher in healing and deliverance into your life but He is the one leading and guiding the process.

3. During the 4th Watch We Meet Jesus the Lover of our Souls.

The Song of Solomon tells the story of a beautiful love affair between a much-despised dark skin slave girl and the ruling King of the land. It is also an allegory of mankind's love relationship with the Godhead. Although we were lowly and despised, He chose us. In the example of the Shulamite woman, we see mankind's desperation and longing to connect with the God of Glory. The 4th Watch is a call to those who are desperate and lovesick. It's a call to them who are desperate for deliverance and desperate for a deeper level of fellowship and communion with the King. It is at the 4th Watch of the morning that the desperate cry out to God and as they do, He reveals Himself to them as the Shepherd King, Jesus the lover of our souls.

4. During the 4th Watch of the Morning Jesus Gives Us an Invitation to Accompany Him to the High Places.

In the example of the Shulamite woman we also see what happens when we don't answer God's call. It was during the 4th Watch that her beloved calls the Shulamite Woman to be with Him in the high places.

My dove in the clefts of the rock,
  in the hiding places on the mountainside,
show me your face,
  let me hear your voice;
for your voice is sweet,
  and your face is lovely.
Catch for us the foxes,
  the little foxes
that ruin the vineyards,
  our vineyards that are in bloom

Song of Solomon 2:14-15

The Shulamite woman is slow to respond when her lover's call and she misses a visitation from the king. The end result, of course, is that she is lovesick for her king. Furthermore, to add injury to insult, an enemy finds her, and she is beaten and abused.

I slept but my heart was awake.
  Listen! My beloved is knocking:
"Open to me, my sister, my darling,
  my dove, my flawless one.
My head is drenched with dew,
  my hair with the dampness of the night."
I have taken off my robe—
  must I put it on again?
I have washed my feet—
  must I soil them again?
My beloved thrust his hand through the latch-opening;
  my heart began to pound for him.
I arose to open for my beloved,
  and my hands dripped with myrrh,
my fingers with flowing myrrh,
  on the handles of the bolt.
I opened for my beloved,
  but my beloved had left; he was gone.
  My heart sank at his departure.
I looked for him but did not find him.
  I called him he did not answer.
The watchmen found me
  as they made their rounds in the city.
They beat me, they bruised me;
  they took away my cloak,
  those watchmen of the walls!

Daughters of Jerusalem, I charge you—
  if you find my beloved,
what will you tell him?
  Tell him I am faint with love.

Song of Solomon 5:2-8

The Shulamite woman is like many of us modern day believers. We don't always answer the call when the Lord wakes us to commune with Him in the middle of the night. Often times we realize, much too late, that it is the Lord Himself calling to us to get out of our beds to come join Him and not the pizza we ate for dinner the night before.

5. The 4th Watch is a Time of Resurrection Power.

Just as the stone was rolled away on Resurrection Sunday during the 4th Watch of the morning, the 4th Watch is a time for the resurrection power of Christ to rise and shine inside of your life. It is a time to resurrect every dormant gift inside of your life. That is why immediately after this watch the sun rises and begins to shine. Oftentimes people are waiting for God to resource them, to put something inside of them that will equip them for the work they believe they are called to do. But did you know that every gift that you have, every gift that you will ever have, has been placed on the inside of you before the foundation of the world? Before you were born. Many of these gifts are buried deep within the bowels of your spiritual belly. As you are trained and activated to release the healing waters on the inside of you, the resurrection power of God will also begin to flow in and through your life and you will begin to see these gifts break forth and manifest in your life.

6. The 4th Watch of the Morning is a Gathering Time of God's Prophetic People.

Prophets love the face of God. They are often love sick for Him, just like the Shulamite woman is in the Song of Solomon. God has a certain relationship with the prophet that is uniquely different from all the other governmental offices. As it relates to His plans He says, "I'll do nothing except I first reveal it to my servant the prophet." (Amos 3:7). It is oftentimes during the night watches that God calls to His prophetic people. Some people will only come to the 4th Watch prayer for a season. This is perfectly acceptable. They will receive the deliverance and or the training they need for their lives and move on. Others, often those called to the prophetic, will find a home there. The 4th Watch is a place where the prophetic people of God gather to be trained and strengthened to operate as a unified voice in the Earth.

7. The Power of Pentecost is Available During the 4th Watch.

The real power of Pentecost is that the people of God where all in the same place, at the same time doing the same thing. They were unified. They met at the time the Lord told them to meet. They met with expectation and understanding that He would send them a gift. So not only were they unified physically they shared a unity of purpose within their minds and spirits. The result of this unity was that they were changed into something else. Peter, who had just days before been too afraid to name himself in the company of Jesus, now begins to take his place as the leader of the church.

8. The 4th Watch is a Time of Miracles.

"Lord, if it's you," Peter replied, "tell me to come to you on the water." "Come," he said. Then Peter got down out of the boat, walked on the water and came toward Jesus. But when he saw the wind, he was afraid and, beginning to

sink, cried out, "Lord, save me!" Immediately Jesus reached out his hand and caught him. "You of little faith," he said, "why did you doubt?" And when they climbed into the boat, the wind died down. Then those who were in the boat worshiped him saying, "truly you are the Son of God."

Matthew 14:28-32

Just like He did for Peter, during the 4th Watch of the morning, Jesus compels us to do the impossible. Jesus is not rebuking Peter in this passage when he asks him, "why did he doubt?" He's instructing him. Peter would go on to do many miraculous things for God. Things that would make walking on water look like small potatoes. Jesus is training Peter on how to break every natural law. Just as He did with Peter, the Lord teaches us how to become practitioners of the supernatural during the 4th Watch.

9. The 4th Watch is a Time of Recompense and Recovery.

As Israel left Egypt, the Lord caused a dreadful fear to come over the Egyptians. So much so, that when the Israelites asked the Egyptians for gold, silver, and articles of clothes, the Egyptians gave up their wealth to the very ones they had held captive. Israel didn't have to strong arm the Egyptians. They simply asked, and the Egyptians gave. It is at the 4th Watch of the morning that the Lord will make your enemies behave. God will do so many exploits on your behalf that the enemy won't even put up a fuss when you ask for your stuff back. Not only will God cause him to return your lost wages, but the evil one will have to recompense you with back pay and damages for pain and suffering.

I've found that one of the first things people usually recover is their voice. Just as Peter was silent when confronted about his relationship with Jesus and rendered voiceless, so many of us have been rendered voiceless in our own personal lives as well. The 4th Watch is a time of recovery. The first and most effective tool the people of God can recover is their voice.

4

The Benefits of Praying During the 4th Watch of the Morning

Then your light will break out like the early morning, and you will soon be healed. Your right and good works will go before you. And the shining-greatness of the Lord will keep watch behind you.

Isaiah 58:8

The 4th Watch of the morning will be a time of great visitation and deliverance. A time of recompense and recovery. A time for believers to sharpen their swords, and be realigned with the purpose, the plans, and the destiny of God for their lives. Jesus, The Commander of the Lord's Army, comes and leads us into the promised territory of our destiny. He shows us how to vanquish all our enemies.

Some of the benefits of praying regularly during the 4th Watch include:

- Deliverance that Remains
- Awakening of a Warrior Spirit

- A Time of Great Visitation from God
- Earthly and Spiritual Re-alignment
- Spiritual, Mental, and Emotional Aptitude to Overcome

5

What Should You Bring with You to the 4th Watch?

Below is a checklist of some tools that you will find useful during the 4th Watch.

Bibles--At some point during the prayer time, God will usually speak to His people through His Word. Every person should have their own Bible. However, it is nice to have multiple versions of the Bible available during times of group study and discussion. Being able to read the scripture in multiple versions helps the people of God get a fuller understanding of what God is doing and saying during your time of prayer.

Pens and Paper-- Although everyone should be taking their own notes in prayer, your group may also want to assign one or more dedicated scribes. The role of the scribe is to write down the Word of the Lord that comes forth during the prayer time. The scribe should also record prayer request, words of prophecy that come forth, as well as prophetic songs and scriptures that come forth during the time of prayer.

Flags and Banners-- During times of high praise and worship, it is fitting and right to raise banners before the King and to offer the Lord what I call, a wave offering. Our prayer team has an array of flags that are set apart as instruments of worship specifically for this purpose. These flags come in a variety of colors. Each color represents different aspects of God's nature. We wave the flags to usher in His presence during times of high praise and worship. We also wave the different color flags in service to God and as an act of intercession. There may be particular times during the service when we want God to show up with His peace, His joy, His power, His deliverance, and so forth. We have a prophet assigned as the Keeper of the Flags. This person oversees, repairs, and is responsible for the acquisition of new flags when necessary. Flags are very easy to make and require limited supplies.

Recording Device-- along with a written account of the Watch, we also make sure our Watch is recorded in various ways. We often tape our meetings using a small audio device that can then be connected to a computer later. The files are then uploaded onto the computer and then placed in a shared file that can be accessed by group members later. This is just another way of being a keeper of what God is saying and doing in the Earth.

Instruments--Like our banners and flags, instruments are also weapons used in our time of worship. If instruments and musicians are not available, feel free to use recorded music. For years, all we had was a CD player and some CDs. And let me tell you, that little CD player took us into the presence of God. Now of course, the reality is you don't need instruments or recorded music to praise the Lord. All you really need is a grateful heart and a voice. Some of our best times of worship have been when the people of God have entered in singing a song a cappella (without the aid of music or instruments) before the Lord. In times like these our whole bodies become instruments of worship before the Lord.

Anointing Oils-- We always make sure we have anointing oils available during our times of prayer. We use a line of anointing oils produced by my company, Abba's Earth Soaps. These oils are formulated from various blends of aromatic and essential oils. However, any oil that has been prayed over and blessed will work too.

A Book of Remembrance – Another form of recording the activity of the 4th Watch is our Book of Remembrance. We have one faithful intercessor who is in charge of this ledger. In this book, the intercessor records the names of the people who were present at the Watch for that morning, any prayer request that came forth, any prophetic words that were spoken forth during our time of prayer, as well as recording the answer to prayers that were prayed at the 4th Watch.

<u>6</u>

Guidelines for Orderly Corporate Prayer

The purpose of this chapter is not to give you a list of do's and don'ts, but to inspire you to pray prophetically. Prophetic prayer is when you come to wait upon the Uncontested Sovereign Ruler of the Universe without a set agenda. You come to see what it is that He wants to accomplish. This does not mean that people cannot and should not come with their own prayer burdens, or requests. They absolutely should! However, they should also come with the understanding that if those particular prayer requests were not specifically addressed during the prayer hour, that as an intercessor and priest, when they went up to meet the Lord in the press that morning, they took every request up with them.

I often instruct the intercessors to take a moment before prayer and write those prayer requests down. Then, as a prophetic act, I ask them to place that piece of paper on their body somewhere. It can be put in a pocket or tucked in a shoe. In a pinch prayer requests can also be written on the palms of your hands. As they go up in the realm of the Spirit to where the Father is, they take those people and those prayer requests too.

Tune your ear to the leader's voice. Whenever you are in corporate prayer, tune your ear to hear the leader's voice. Whether that's the person leading the prayer group or another individual God has alighted upon and is using at the moment. With twelve or more voices in a room, things can get very loud pretty fast. You must learn to listen for the sound of the leader. This is a very important principle—just as you must learn to hear the still quiet voice of the Lord in the midst of chaos, so in corporate prayer must you learn to hear the voice of the leader above the crowd.

Recognize the shifts of God. We should all know what it sounds like when the Spirit of the Lord alights upon someone's voice. We should all know what it sounds like when we've expired a place in the spirit realm and the Lord is calling us up higher. This is a type of hearing and sensitivity that is developed over time as you pray.

Ascend in an orderly fashion. March in an orderly fashion. When we gather together God may give one a song, another a word, and still another an interpretation. We can all prophesy in turn and in the spirit of order. The spirit of the prophet is subject to the prophet. If God is saying something to you and there is not a space for it yet—write it down. Don't worry, it's not a cup of milk it won't expire.

Trust is absolutely key. You have to trust that this is the place that God has brought you to, that these are the people he has connected you to pray with, and that the one leading the group is the one He has ordained to lead. If you have doubts, issues, problems, or reservations about any of the above, I beseech you in love to have a conversation or if need be, take some time away from the prayer group, get to know the leader or the individuals in question in a different kind of setting. But please don't do the religious thing and just keep coming without dealing with the issue. That would only hinder the work of the ministry. Don't let offenses build, deal with them quickly. Offense breaks down trust. Scripture tells us plainly two cannot walk together unless they agree. If you don't trust the leader, you will not follow where they are going, and if you can't trust your sister or brother who is praying next to you, we won't go up.

Come with an expectation of power. Those that know the Lord shall be strong and do exploits (Daniel 11:32). Please don't come because you think that the 4th Watch is the latest, happening prayer circle in town. It's not, this is just one group. God has many powerful groups. Come because God has told you to come. Come bringing power, come expecting to meet power.

No lone rangers in corporate prayer. Follow the flow. If everybody else is crying, you should not be laughing. There is a religious spirit that often tries to attack intercessors who engage in corporate prayer. This spirit tells the intercessor that the leader is off track, and everybody else is off track too. We must be careful that we don't get tripped up by this spirit. It comes to breed disunity and it immediately stops the move of God. When you walk into a room for a corporate prayer gathering this devil is usually the first one there.

Fight for unity. Because the body of Christ is so dismembered today by different ideas, and beliefs, we must fight for oneness. Your greatest battle as a prayer team will be the battle to remain on one accord. Scripture tells us in Acts 2, that when the people of God were all in one place on one accord, the power of Pentecost fell upon them. Our oneness will bring the presence of God with power and great authority, so we must contend for this.

This is not a spectator's sport. When you come into a corporate gathering, you must be prepared to press your way into the presence of God no matter what. This is important because in a corporate setting everybody in the room has mass and takes up space. This is true in the natural realm, and it's true in the spirit realm as well. Corporate unity requires each one of us to push past ourselves, our issues and feelings. In order to "go up" to where the Father is, we all must press to get there. I cannot emphasize enough that everyone has got to pull their own weight in the spirit realm. That being said, the 4th Watch is not a forum for the unconvinced or the mere curious. This is a space for the convinced and the desperate. If you find yourself in either of those two categories—curious, or unconvinced, I encourage you to seek out a class or study on prayer, but do not hinder the move of God with non- participation.

Come dressed for battle. Wear comfortable clothes, show up with the right tools. You wouldn't come to a gun fight with out a gun, please don't show up to prayer without your Bible. A notebook dedicated solely to prayer as well as pens, pencils, and highlighters would be helpful as well. We are each accountable for every Word the Father speaks to us in prayer. As the Lord begins to speak, make sure you write His declarations and proclamations down. He expects His Word to be properly dispatched and recorded in the Earth. There should be a designated scribe or scribes. As I mentioned earlier, in our prayer circle, we have scribes that record by writing and others who audio record our times of prayer. However, even if you do have someone assigned to the position of scribe, everyone should be keeping a personal log of the things God is saying and doing during your prayer times.

Come prepared to knock on Heaven's door. Learn to wait on the King of Glory. Wait for the move of the Spirit. That means if the prayer starts at three o'clock and the Wind of the Holy Spirit still hasn't blown through by 4, you don't conjure up something. You wait on the Lord with worship and thanksgiving. Until He decides to show up.

Always leave time for sharing and discussion. I have two rules for those who pray in our circle. The first rule is: **what is shared here stays here and what's learned here leaves here.** Because this is a place where people are coming to receive deliverance, this should be a confidential space. We don't discuss what happens at the 4th Watch with people who weren't at the 4th Watch. We invite people to come and experience the Watch for themselves. The second rule is: **nobody leaves with our stuff.** What I mean by that is this: oftentimes in prayer, people think the revelation they received is personal and not for the group. You didn't go up into the press alone, you broke through with an entire group of people. Therefore, the revelation you received is not just yours alone, it belongs to the entire group of people. To the victor goes the spoils of war.

7

How Should One Prepare for the 4TH Watch?

If you have decided to meet the Lord at the 4th Watch of the morning simply start by being intentional about it. Set an alarm clock. Go to bed early. Wake up in the morning excited and come to the prayer time with the expectation that you will encounter God's power. Most importantly remember this one thing: **an *invitation from God is not a common thing, it's a holy thing.***

Myself, and the intercessors who pray with me at the 4th Watch of the morning, do so because this is the Watch that God called our body of believers to in 2007. We did not choose this prayer hour because we are morning people. Trust me, on the contrary, many of us are not! We answered the call to come, by invitation of the King because we are soldiers in His army. One thing you can be assured of this, when God calls you to a particular Watch for any extended period of time, He will give you the grace to do it.

Intercessors do themselves and the Kingdom of God a great dis-service by randomly choosing a prayer hour that is convenient for the people. Middle Eastern Culture understood what we in our modern-day American culture have yet to understand. It is foolish and futile to come uninvited before a great King.

8

How Can You Bring the 4TH Watch To Your Church or City?

Start with the prophets and the prophetic-like folks. Prophets are often drawn to prayer ministry like eagles are to a flowing water source. Secondly, gather a group of committed intercessors together. This group can be a combination of those who are seasoned prayer warriors and those who know very little about prayer but have a heart for prayer. What's most important at this stage is commitment.

Next, set up an appointment with your pastor and or the leadership team over your ministry to talk about hosting your 4th Watch prayer time at the church. When you sit down with the leadership, be sure to discuss the logistics of hosting a prayer gathering in the middle of the night. Will you be needing keys to the church for an early morning prayer? Or is there someone from ministry staff with a key that will meet you? What type of neighborhood is your church in? This is important because you'll need to know whether to keep the doors of the church locked and simply open the door when people from your prayer circle come, or if you should unlock the doors of the church and just leave them open during the duration of the prayer. In the summer, will you need air conditioning? In the winter, will you need to be able to adjust and regulate the heat? What about the church parking lot, is it well lit? Will you see or hear members of your prayer circle when they come out for prayer? What about when people show up late? How will you advertise this to the body of Christ? Will it be open to just the people in your church or will you open it up to believers around your city?

There are a ton of details to consider, I know. Some of them are a pain in the neck, but the benefits that you, your church, your family, your community, our nation and our world will see when the people of God began to gather together for corporate prayer, are most definitely worth it.

Lastly, we'd be happy to come and do a training with you and your team to help you get your 4th Watch off the ground. To book Minister Sparkman contact Kubernesis Administrative Services on behalf of the Ironer's Press. Telephone:1-858-663-7810, you can also contact us via email: kubernesis.info@gmail.com

For additional questions that were not answered in this manual, please contact the author at doingbusinesswithgod@gmail.com

APPENDIX A

Glossary of Terms Used In Intercession

On the following pages you will find a list of terms that I often use when praying. If you attend a 4th Watch with me or the intercessors who pray with me, you will hear many of these terms on a regular basis. Some of these are general words that anyone would use in prayer and some of these are words that I myself have created to describe what is going on in the realm of the Spirit as we go up.

Alight upon-- Oftentimes, when praying with a group of believers, God will place a spotlight on someone's voice. When that happens, we say that the Spirit of God has alighted on them. He wants to use them to carry the prayer baton so to speak, for that moment. All the people in the meeting may be praying at the same volume but you will hear a shift, to let you know that God is doing something particularly with that one person's voice. The others in the group should fall back and allow the voice that the Spirit has alighted upon to come forth to bring forth the prayer, the song, the word of prophecy or whatever else the Lord wants to bring forth.

Be Free in the Holy Spirit--The phrase Be Free in the Holy Spirit is a call to remove your personal inhibitions. Most people feel uncomfortable when they come to pray in a circle for the first time. They don't want to be out of order or move out of turn and often, in an attempt to regard protocol, they quench and hinder the Holy Spirit operating inside of them. When you hear the call, "Be free in the Holy Spirit," that means go ahead relax and allow the Holy Spirit to use you and flow through you in whatever way He deems appropriate.

It never fails, when we have the talk back portion of our prayer and I ask the question, "Did you press all the way in this morning? Did you totally empty yourself out on the altar before God?" There will always be at least one or two brave souls who dare to be honest, who say, "I could have pressed in farther. Or they may say something like, "I felt the Lord telling me to do this or that, but I didn't." When I ask the question, "Why not?" they say something to the effect of, "Well, it felt strange to do that and I didn't want to be out of order." The only way to be out of order in prayer is to not give God what He asks for. Don't worry about offending people or looking strange. We are all trying to get to where the Father would have us to go. The invitation to be Free in the Holy Ghost is an invitation to both freedom and order. If you allow God to completely use you, He won't let you get out of order.

Bind-- To tie with ropes or cords, to prohibit something from acting.

Bring Forth-- Come out of the shadows, trust the Spirit of God who has alighted upon your voice and bring forth whatever He would have you to bring.

Build a Platform--This is what the other's in the prayer circle do when the Spirit of the Lord alights upon a particular person's voice. The others in the prayer circle fall back. However, they should not become totally quiet or disengaged when they hear the Lord alight upon a fellow team member's voice. They simply become quieter as they undergird the person who is leading the charge in prayer. As they add their agreement to the prayer in the form of an, Amen, yes, or so be it, as well as praying in their heavenly language, they build a platform underneath the lead person praying. This platform helps to press that person further into the realm of the Spirit so that their prayer, which started off by faith, can now take on the mind and nature of what Christ wants prayed into the Earth.

Burden—or prayer burden is the thing that weighs on the heart that must pray for. It is the weight that we feel when God has called us to pray for something in the Earth. Sometimes, intercessors will experience the burden as a physical pressing in their bodies that makes them uncomfortable. This uncomfortable feeling is a physical reminder that God is calling the intercessor to pray for a situation. Sometimes, the intercessor will even take on the physical pains of another. Their job is to hand the burden over to the Lord through prayer. (See Disband the Burden)

Come Forth-- (See Bring Forth) Make your voice louder. Let the sound flow from your belly with assurance and clarity.

Decree-- Is a law that you make. There is a realm that we, the people of God, can enter in prayer where we don't pray and ask God to do or accomplish things for us. In this realm, which I call the realm of Declatory Grace, we decide a thing, God hands us His signet ring (His stamp of approval) and what we say it shall be. When we write new laws, we call these decrees.

Declaration-- Is the proclamation, or the verbal speaking forth of the written decree. As it is declared, spoken out loud through the prophetic intercessor, the decree is published in both the Heavens and the Earth.

Disband--Disbanding the burden refers to the intercessors responsibility to make a heavenly transfer of the prayer burdens. In other words, you pray about it and leave it in the hands of the Lord. You don't hold the weight of the thing, not in your mind, body, or heart. You don't worry or fret over it. Instead, you pray until the burden is lifted. If the burden is not properly disbanded, although spiritual in nature, it can sit on the physical body and cause problems for the intercessor. Praying until the burden is completely lifted is called disbanding the burden.

Establish--When a decree is spoken and declared in the Earth, we say that it has been established or accomplished. It is the job of the intercessor to accomplish, or see, that the will of Heaven is established in the Earth.

Loose -- To unbind, cause to flow, set free.

Press-- Intentional intense prayer. The press is how we go up to where the Father is. As the intercessor goes up in the realm of the Spirit, the intercessors must press themselves past demonic forces that would not want the intercessor passing through their territory. This struggle of trying to get to where the Father is creates the press.

A Prophetic Act--A physical action done by faith during times of prayer that may make the person doing the act feel foolish, but nevertheless, if done by faith, can have lifelong implications. Example of a prophetic act maybe the Lord telling you to march, twirl, wave a flag, or perhaps release certain sounds.

Prophetic Song--Prophetic songs often come forth in corporate prayer. New songs which we are to sing to the Lord. Oftentimes the Lord will sing back a response to His people. This is Zephaniah 3:17 in action:

> *The Lord your God in your midst,*
> *The Mighty One, will save;*
> *He will rejoice over you with gladness,*
> *He will quiet you with His love,*
> *He will rejoice over you with singing"*

The Lord comes into our midst to shower us with His love and to sing over His people. We want these new prophetic songs to come forth because deliverance always accompanies them. Also the very act of singing itself, helping with learning and retention, God will often sing over His people as a way to help us to remember His promises.

Rubble--Refers to the emotional and spiritual waste and wreckage in a person's life. It's the old things left over in our lives. Demons, emotional, and psychological baggage, woundedness and generational curses.

Shift--Shifts in the Spirit can be subtle or major changes in the flow of direction during the prayer. The ability to recognize shifts is developed over time as you become more sensitive to the Holy Spirit's leading. It is necessary to understand the shifts so that you receive all God has for you during the prayer time.

Undergird--To secure or fasten from the underside, as with rope or chains. When you undergird in prayer, you support the individual who is leading by coming underneath them and pressing them forward. In other words, you should not be praying so loud as to overtake or override the lead person, who is oftentimes, by the way, searching to hear where God is taking them next. You should pray in such a way that you press them forward but yet at the same time don't disrupt what God is doing in and through them. (Also see Building a Platform).

Weight--Refers to the spiritual mass that every person has. A person's spiritual mass has nothing to do with their physical size in the natural realm, and everything to do with the call of God on their lives. The greater the call and the appointment, the more weight that person carries in the realm of the Spirit. Oftentimes in prayer, I meet intercessors who have no idea who they are, much less the amount of weight they carry. These saints usually become easy prey for the enemy who has convinced them to undervalue their worth. When they come into a corporate prayer setting these believers often think they have nothing to give and thus they end up weighing down the meeting with their lack of participation. Taking a group of people up in corporate prayer is like flying a jumbo jet airplane. The job of the pilot is to get the entire group of people to lift off the ground at the same time. Everyone needs to pull their weight in the realm of the Spirit in order to make this happen.

APPENDIX B

The History of Biblical Anointing Oils & Why We Should Use Them Today

Is anyone among you sick? Let them call the elders of the church to pray over them and anoint them with oil in the name of the Lord. And the prayer offered in faith will make the sick person well; the Lord will raise them up. If they have sinned, they will be forgiven. Therefore, confess your sins to each other and pray for each other so that you may be healed. The prayer of a righteous person is powerful and effective.

James 5:14-16

The word anointing actually means to smear with oil or ointment. In Biblical days, it was fully understood that when the scripture in James 5 says, "let the sick call for the elders to anoint them with oil and pray over them," that the oil the elders used would not just be vegetable oil. Everyone understood that the oil being used was a combination of natural healing plants infused into a carrier oil such as olive oil which was plenteously available in that region of the world.

The elder's prayer of faith and the healing aromatic components of the oils worked together in synergy to heal the individual coming for prayer. Because antibiotics had not yet been discovered at the time, all people groups of the Earth relied on aromatic plants and prayers to whatever deity they served heal themselves. The people of God just had the wisdom to know that there was only one prayer of faith that could heal that's the one prayed to Jehovah Rapha, our Healer.

AROMATHERAPY IN THE BIBLE

The Bible refers to essential oils or aromatic plants over 1000 times. In fact, God is the first aromatherapist. In Exodus chapter 30, God gives Moses the recipe for the holy anointing oil that would be used to anoint the priest and all the instruments used in the tabernacle.

Essential oils are very expensive now and they were very expensive in Biblical days. Because of the extremely high cost of aromatic plant oils, essential oils were only used by royalty and the very wealthiest people in society. So when the wise men presented the Baby Jesus, with Frankincense and Myrrh (both considered the most valuable of all essential oils for both their aroma and healing properties) they were recognizing Jesus's Sovereign Lordship. In

Biblical days these two oils would only be found in royal palaces.

The healing properties of essential oils were legendary. No one had to tell their users how to apply them. For example, Mary would have known that she could rub Myrrh on her belly to heal her stretch marks and that the scent of the oil would be calming and comforting to her infant child when she nursed him. Also no one would have had to tell her to use Frankincense to protect her baby both from natural predators like viruses and from supernatural predators like demons, because the people of that time period understood the aromatic properties of the plant would ward these enemies off.

The Old Testament priest also practiced aromatherapy. Leviticus chapter fourteen tells us that the priest would apply oil to the right tip of the earlobe of the one being cleansed, on the thumb of his right hand, and on the big toe of his right foot—all points on the body where aromatic oils could be easily absorbed into the bloodstream.

Mary of Bethany anointed Jesus with Spikenard. She anointed His head and his feet. Jesus said she did this to prepare Him for his death and burial. Many of the components within Spikenard have the ability to heal old wounds. The oil also carries along with it the ability to prepare a person spiritually, mentally and emotionally for a difficult challenge. How beautiful for the Father to inspire Mary to do this for our Lord right before He would endure the greatest fight of His natural life.

ABBA'S EARTH ANOINTING OILS

If you have experienced my ministry, you know that oftentimes I minister with oils. What most people don't know is that those oils are all blends that the Father gave me.

I discovered the healing ministry of aromatherapy and essential oils during my college years. At the time, I began to study everything I could about the healing nature of plants and their effects on the body.

One day, I received a box shipped to my home by mail by a very reputable company that I had often ordered from in the past. The box contained an array of precious very costly essential oils. I knew that there was no way I could afford the oils in that box and that there had to have been a mistake. Even still, I couldn't help opening the box and smelling the precious bottles within. I called the company because the box contained several hundreds of dollars' worth of oil and I didn't want to receive a bill. I was told by the company to keep the oils as a gift. I am convinced that the gift came from the Father who wanted me to learn how to use these wonderful oils.

Today, all of Abba's Earth Anointing Oils are a blend of the finest, therapeutic grade essential oils mixed in a natural vegetable oil base. Each oil in our line has an accompanying scripture verse to pray and stand on as you use the oil. Always pray and ask God which oil you should use whenever praying and anointing yourself or others.

Whenever anointing myself or anyone else with Abba's Earth Anointing Oils the first thing I do is dab a little bit of oil into the palm of my hand and cup my hands over my nose and breathe deeply. I do this because the molecules in essential oils are small enough to past the blood brain barrier. When we breathe them in, they go directly into the bloodstream and heal the way they are sent forth to do. Fragrance oils created in a laboratory by man cannot do this. Only the pure plant oils created by God the Father have the ability to heal.

You can order our oils by emailing us at doingbusinesswithgod@gmail.com

ABBA'S EARTH ANOINTING OILS

FIRE

A blend of Clove, Cinnamon, Frankincense, Peppermint, Eucalyptus, Red Thyme and Cedarwood Essential oils and Extra Virgin Olive oil. Use Fire to burn out physical and spiritual impurities. Fire Scripture verse Matthew 3:11: *I baptize you with water for repentance, but he who is coming after me is mightier than I, whose sandals I am not worthy to carry. He will baptize you with the Holy Spirit and fire.*

PEACE

Lavender, Patchouli, Ylang Ylang, and Myrrh essential oils and Extra Virgin Olive Oil. The aromatic oils in this blend are soothing, antiseptic, and in combination, they act as a mild nerve sedative and a natural anti-depressant. Use Peace to combat spiritual, physical, and emotional effects of fear, anxiety & depression. Peace Scripture verse Numbers 6:25-26: *The LORD make his face shine upon you and be gracious to you; the LORD turn his face toward you and give you peace."*

JOY

Orange, Grapefruit, Ylang Ylang, and Myrrh essential oils and Olive oil. The oils used in this blend are anti-depressant, antiseptic, useful for insomnia, nervous depression, anger and rage. Use the oil of Joy to fight against heaviness of heart, and for intercessors who have trouble disbanding spiritual burdens. Joy scripture verse is Psalms 5:11-12: *But let all who take refuge in you rejoice; let them ever sing for joy, and spread your protection over them, that those who love your name may exult in you. For you bless the righteous, O LORD; you cover him with favor as with a shield.*

INTIMACY

Spikenard, Lavender essential oil, olive oil. Spikenard is the precious and costly aromatic that Mary of Bethany used to anoint Christ's feet with. It regulates the heartbeat, kills staph infections, and wounds that will not heal. Use this pleasant aroma to draw you into the presence of God. Intimacy scripture verse is **Zephaniah 3:17:** *the Lord your God is in your midst, a mighty one who will save, he will rejoice over you with gladness, he will quiet you by his love; he will exult over you with loud singing.*

BREAKER

Essential oils of Peppermint, Tea Tree, Eucalyptus, Lavender Essential oil and Olive oil. Use Breaker to fight against physical (viral infections), spiritual infirmities such as generational curses, demonic attacks. The scripture verse for Breaker is Psalm 103: 1-4: *Bless the Lord, O my soul, and all that is within me, bless his holy name! Bless the Lord, O my soul, and forget not all his benefits, who forgives all your iniquity, who heals all your diseases, who redeems your life from the pit.*

THE PRIESTHOOD

Essential oils of Myrrh, Cassia, Cinnamon, Calamus and Olive oil. A replica of the oils used in Exodus chapter 30. This blend was given to Moses by God to be used to anoint the priest and the sacred articles used in service to God. God specified that this oil should never be poured on an "ordinary" person but to be reserved for the priest. Since we are now a nation of kings and priests, we can use this blend. Use this blend anytime you are preparing to enter a time of intercession, worship or ministry to the people. Let it be a sweet fragrant offering to the Father as you minister before him. The scripture for

Priesthood oil is Exodus 30: 22-30: *Then the LORD said to Moses, "Take the following fine spices: 500 shekels of liquid myrrh, half as much (that is, 250 shekels) of fragrant cinnamon, 250 shekels of fragrant calamus, 500 shekels of cassia—all according to the sanctuary shekel— and a hin of olive oil. Make these into a sacred anointing oil, a fragrant blend, the work of a perfumer. It will be the sacred anointing oil. Then use it to anoint the tent of meeting, the ark of the covenant law, the table and all its articles, the lampstand and its accessories, the altar of incense, the altar of burnt offering and all its utensils, and the basin with its stand. You shall consecrate them, so they will be most holy, and whatever touches them will be holy. "Anoint Aaron and his sons and consecrate them so they may serve me as priests."*

COURAGE

Essential oils of Orange, Cloves, and Peppermint are used in this formulation. Orange fights against fear and anxiety while Peppermint soothes the stomach, and Cloves strengthen the heart. Courage scripture verse is Deuteronomy 31:6: *Be strong and of good courage, do not fear nor be afraid of them; for the LORD your God,*

He is the One who goes with you. He will not leave you nor forsake you.

WOUNDS

A blend of Spikenard, Hyssops, Frankincense, Cassia, and Cedar essential oils. Use to heal physical as well as spiritual brokenness, particularly childhood wounds. The scripture verse for Wounds oil is Psalm 147:3: *He heals the brokenhearted and binds up their wounds.*

BEAUTY FOR ASHES

Lavender, Rosemary, Cedar, & Thyme essential oils in a jojoba oil blend. Use Beauty for Ashes when praying for recompense & recovery after spiritual and physical loss. This oil blend is particularly suited to fight against hair loss. The scripture verse for Beauty for Ashes is Isaiah 61:1-3: *The Spirit of the Sovereign LORD is on me, because the LORD has anointed me to proclaim good news to the poor. He has sent me to bind up the brokenhearted, to proclaim freedom for the captives and release from darkness for the prisoners, to proclaim the year of the LORD's favor and the day of vengeance of our God, to comfort all who mourn, and provide for those who grieve in Zion—to bestow on them a crown of beauty instead of ashes.*

PROTECTION

A blend of Frankincense and Myrrh in an Extra Virgin Olive Oil carrier base. When used together, Frankincense and Myrrh combine their strengths to become: antiseptic, anti-fungal, anti-inflammatory, and anti-depressant. These oils are oxygenating to the body tissues and support the immune system by enhancing the body's natural defense. Helpful in combat against fear, stress, and frustration. Use this oil when praying a prayer covering for physical, mental, emotional and or spiritual protection. The scripture verse for Protection is Psalm 91:1-8: *Whoever dwells in the shelter of the Most High will rest in the shadow of the Almighty. I will say of the LORD, "He is my refuge and my fortress, my God, in whom I trust. Surely he will save you from the fowler's snare and from the deadly pestilence. He will cover you with his feathers and under his wings you will find refuge; his faithfulness will be your shield and rampart. You will not fear the terror of night, nor the arrow that flies by day, nor the pestilence that stalks in the darkness, nor the plague that destroys at midday. A thousand may fall at your side, ten thousand at your right hand, but it will not come near you. You will only observe with your eyes and see the punishment of the wicked.*

Appendix C

Watch Notes

This next section is a log for all your 4th Watch notes. Assuming you meet once a week, you will have enough journal space for the first year of your time at the Watch. It's not just the scribes job to record what God is doing. It's everyone's job to record what God is doing. One of the ways we can do this, is by keeping a written record of the themes, scriptures, prophetic words, and observations, people saw— this includes sensory experiences such as taste and smell as well.

Watch Notes

Date:
Theme/ Lesson:
Scripture verses:

Prophetic Words:

Observations:

Watch Notes

Date:
Theme/ Lesson:
Scripture verses:

Prophetic Words:

Observations:

Watch Notes

Date:
Theme/ Lesson:
Scripture verses:

Prophetic Words:

Observations:

Watch Notes

Date:
Theme/ Lesson:
Scripture verses:

Prophetic Words:

Observations:

Watch Notes

Date:
Theme/ Lesson:
Scripture verses:

Prophetic Words:

Observations:

Watch Notes

Date:
Theme/ Lesson:
Scripture verses:

Prophetic Words:

Observations:

Watch Notes

Date:
Theme/ Lesson:
Scripture verses:

Prophetic Words:

Observations:

Watch Notes

Date:
Theme/ Lesson:
Scripture verses:

Prophetic Words:

Observations:

Watch Notes

Date:
Theme/ Lesson:
Scripture verses:

Prophetic Words:

Observations:

Watch Notes

Date:
Theme/ Lesson:
Scripture verses:

Prophetic Words:

Observations:

Watch Notes

Date:
Theme/ Lesson:
Scripture verses:

Prophetic Words:

Observations:

Watch Notes

Date:
Theme/ Lesson:
Scripture verses:

Prophetic Words:

Observations:

Watch Notes

Date:
Theme/ Lesson:
Scripture verses:

Prophetic Words:

Observations:

Watch Notes

Date:
Theme/ Lesson:
Scripture verses:

Prophetic Words:

Observations:

Watch Notes

Date:
Theme/ Lesson:
Scripture verses:

Prophetic Words:

Observations:

Watch Notes

Date:
Theme/ Lesson:
Scripture verses:

Prophetic Words:

Observations:

<u>Watch Notes</u>

Date:
Theme/ Lesson:
Scripture verses:

Prophetic Words:

Observations:

Watch Notes

Date:
Theme/ Lesson:
Scripture verses:

Prophetic Words:

Observations:

Watch Notes

Date:
Theme/ Lesson:
Scripture verses:

Prophetic Words:

Observations:

Watch Notes

Date:
Theme/ Lesson:
Scripture verses:

Prophetic Words:

Observations:

Watch Notes

Date:
Theme/ Lesson:
Scripture verses:

Prophetic Words:

Observations:

Watch Notes

Date:
Theme/ Lesson:
Scripture verses:

Prophetic Words:

Observations:

Watch Notes

Date:
Theme/ Lesson:
Scripture verses:

Prophetic Words:

Observations:

Watch Notes

Date:
Theme/ Lesson:
Scripture verses:

Prophetic Words:

Observations:

Watch Notes

Date:
Theme/ Lesson:
Scripture verses:

Prophetic Words:

Observations:

Watch Notes

Date:
Theme/ Lesson:
Scripture verses:

Prophetic Words:

Observations:

Watch Notes

Date:
Theme/ Lesson:
Scripture verses:

Prophetic Words:

Observations:

Watch Notes

Date:
Theme/ Lesson:
Scripture verses:

Prophetic Words:

Observations:

Watch Notes

Date:
Theme/ Lesson:
Scripture verses:

Prophetic Words:

Observations:

Watch Notes

Date:
Theme/ Lesson:
Scripture verses:

Prophetic Words:

Observations:

Watch Notes

Date:
Theme/ Lesson:
Scripture verses:

Prophetic Words:

Observations:

Watch Notes

Date:
Theme/ Lesson:
Scripture verses:

Prophetic Words:

Observations:

Watch Notes

Date:
Theme/ Lesson:
Scripture verses:

Prophetic Words:

Observations:

Watch Notes

Date:
Theme/ Lesson:
Scripture verses:

Prophetic Words:

Observations:

Watch Notes

Date:
Theme/ Lesson:
Scripture verses:

Prophetic Words:

Observations:

Watch Notes

Date:
Theme/ Lesson:
Scripture verses:

Prophetic Words:

Observations:

Watch Notes

Date:
Theme/ Lesson:
Scripture verses:

Prophetic Words:

Observations:

Watch Notes

Date:
Theme/ Lesson:
Scripture verses:

Prophetic Words:

Observations:

Watch Notes

Date:
Theme/ Lesson:
Scripture verses:

Prophetic Words:

Observations:

Watch Notes

Date:
Theme/ Lesson:
Scripture verses:

Prophetic Words:

Observations:

Watch Notes

Date:
Theme/ Lesson:
Scripture verses:

Prophetic Words:

Observations:

Watch Notes

Date:
Theme/ Lesson:
Scripture verses:

Prophetic Words:

Observations:

Watch Notes

Date:
Theme/ Lesson:
Scripture verses:

Prophetic Words:

Observations:

Watch Notes

Date:
Theme/ Lesson:
Scripture verses:

Prophetic Words:

Observations:

Watch Notes

Date:
Theme/ Lesson:
Scripture verses:

Prophetic Words:

Observations:

Watch Notes

Date:
Theme/ Lesson:
Scripture verses:

Prophetic Words:

Observations:

Watch Notes

Date:
Theme/ Lesson:
Scripture verses:

Prophetic Words:

Observations:

Watch Notes

Date:
Theme/ Lesson:
Scripture verses:

Prophetic Words:

Observations:

Watch Notes

Date:
Theme/ Lesson:
Scripture verses:

Prophetic Words:

Observations:

Watch Notes

Date:
Theme/ Lesson:
Scripture verses:

Prophetic Words:

Observations:

Watch Notes

Date:
Theme/ Lesson:
Scripture verses:

Prophetic Words:

Observations:

www.ingramcontent.com/pod-product-compliance
Lightning Source LLC
Chambersburg PA
CBHW020143130526
44591CB00030B/190